AUDIO
ACCESS
INCLUDED

PLAYBACK+
Speed • Pitch • Balance • Loop

CLASSIC **TROMBONE** POP SONGS

Audio arrangements by Peter Deneff

To access audio visit:
www.halleonard.com/mylibrary

Enter Code
6316-2597-0067-6725

ISBN 978-1-5400-0249-5

7777 W. BLUEMOUND RD. P.O. BOX 13819 MILWAUKEE, WI 53213

Visit Hal Leonard Online at
www.halleonard.com

BRIDGE OVER TROUBLED WATER

TROMBONE

Words and Music by
PAUL SIMON

CANDLE IN THE WIND

TROMBONE

Words and Music by ELTON JOHN
and BERNIE TAUPIN

DUST IN THE WIND

TROMBONE

Words and Music by
KERRY LIVGREN

4

EVERY BREATH YOU TAKE

TROMBONE

Music and Lyrics by
STING

FIRE AND RAIN

TROMBONE

Words and Music by
JAMES TAYLOR

HAVE I TOLD YOU LATELY

TROMBONE

Words and Music by
VAN MORRISON

Slowly, with feeling

Piano

GOOD VIBRATIONS

TROMBONE

Words and Music by BRIAN WILSON
and MIKE LOVE

HEAVEN

TROMBONE

Words and Music by BRYAN ADAMS
and JIM VALLANCE

13

LEAN ON ME

TROMBONE

Words and Music by
BILL WITHERS

D.S. al Coda

CODA

f

1.

2.

SHE'S ALWAYS A WOMAN

TROMBONE

Words and Music by
BILLY JOEL

To Coda

D.S. al Coda

CODA

rit.

WITH A LITTLE HELP FROM MY FRIENDS

TROMBONE

Words and Music by JOHN LENNON
and PAUL McCARTNEY

TEARS IN HEAVEN

TROMBONE

Words and Music by ERIC CLAPTON
and WILL JENNINGS